Thanks for everything

Realization has to be followed by realignment.

Manish Patel

SECOND CHILDHOOD | 2 | Manish Patel

SECOND CHILDHOOD

MANISH PATEL

If you've purchased this book without a cover, you should be aware this book may have been stolen property and reported as "unsold and destroyed" by the publisher. In such case, the author has not received any payment for this "stripped" book.

Copyright © November 2011 by Manish Patel

All rights reserved. The book is based on true events. No part of this book may be reproduced by any form or by electronic means, including for information storage and retrieval systems, without written permission from the author, except by a reviewer who may quote brief passages in a review.

Publisher
Sadie Books, 215 E Camden Ave, H-11,
Moorestown, NJ 08057
856-313-0548
Sadie-books.com

ISBN-10: 0-9816047-7-3
ISBN-13: 978-0-9816047-7-0

Library of Congress Control #: 2011938008

Cover Design: www.iovista.com
Layout: callendesign.com

Author Website: www.thesecondchildhood.com

Dedication

I would like to dedicate this book to my dear friend Shreeraj and my dear patient Loriene Marie Scherbak. When I lost Shreeraj, I started thinking about the purpose of life. Thinking led to penning a book based on Shreeraj's love for others. Shreeraj believed that we should treat each other as best friends. He understood that we are all connected and there is a reason for everything. I wondered, at times, if God sent him to me so that I would be propelled to take up the cause of writing this book.

It breaks my heart to write about Shreeraj because I miss Shreeraj greatly. Though his loss is devastating, he taught me to accept whatever life gives me, and to embrace it wholeheartedly. It is Shreeraj that I pour into Second Childhood, to inspire you to absorb his passion for life. His moral values guide us to show people love, care and affection, while protecting them from hazard, and providing them with a sense of security.

Shreeraj's devotion to mental and spiritual insight drew many people to him. I had the honor of sharing 14 years of my life with Shreeraj. He taught me how to hold on to life and be optimistic through every situation, for better or for worse. It is his personality that comes through this book. His ideas and inspiration make it possible; his selfless gifts of love form the basis of these words.

One of my undertakings is to share the importance of spreading love to everyone in our lives, especially our parents. We may never be able to pay back our parents for all that they have given us, but our honest efforts and thoughts will always count for something good.

About a month before I published this book, I attended Marie's funeral. Marie is one of the reasons for decoding the phrase "once a man and twice a child".

It broke my heart since I could not see her when I visited her home just a month before she died. I learned from her daughter that she was in hospital, when I went to see her.

I was glad to be a part of her 100th birthday party, where she recognized me in front of her family, in spite of her memory loss. She even remembered my elder son's name, at that time. A week after her funeral, her daughter, Pat, visited my office with two little cute pillows stating that her mom bought them for my kids. Her mom had wanted to deliver the pillows, but she passed before she could visit. I almost cried because of her love and affection for my family and me.

Marie lived 100 years in the world, but she will live forever in my heart. Marie became one of my patients when she had a left knee replacement at the age of 96. I will never forget the beautiful smile she gave me, though she had postoperative pain and stiffness. About a year later, Marie had right knee surgery, and she requested me as her physical therapist. After that, I saw her a few times following hospitalizations.

Shreeraj and Marie taught me that all we put out always comes back to us; it is the law of the universe. Every action has an opposite and equal reaction. To God, actions count.

In Memory of Shreeraj

1974-2009

In Memory of Loriene Marie Scherbak

1911-2011

SECOND CHILDHOOD | 15 | Manish Patel

A Gift From Lucille

Every morning, the cup and saucer silently remind me that this is a day where I will not just work and do my job. Each day, I will work to do my part to serve elders and those around me.

It is my mission to create strong relationships with people, and do my part to leave the world a better place than I found it.

Lucille is the inspiration for Chapter 7 of this book, on the topic of Relationships.

Manish Patel

Acknowledgements

First and foremost, I thank God. It is with God's grace that I have been able to write Second Childhood. I am also grateful to my parents for their continuous blessing and guidance.

I thank God for a great dad. Despite a busy physician calendar, he took special interest in this book while helping make needed changes. My mom is the reason for my existence, and I cannot thank her enough for everything.

I thank my wife, Ripal, and my two sons, Ayush and Ishan. It has taken a long time to see this book through to fruition. The time I spent on it was time away from my family. I could never have written it without all of their never-ending support, patience and understanding.

I thank Komal Patel, who translated my words and ideas to compose this book you are about to read. I thank my close friend, Milap Patel, for his support and guidance. He designed the cover art and the website, and he has been an integral part of arranging this book. I thank my very good friend Heart Desai for his belief in my book. I would also like to thank my dad's best friend Ramesh Mehta for his valuable advice for this book. I thank Cassandra Allen for her support in taking this project from a manuscript to a book.

Last but not least, I would like to thank my best friend Shreeraj. He was my closest friend, and his life served as the inspiration for this book.

Thank you.

Manish Patel

Table of Contents

1 Inspiration 27

2 Question: Quest on 37

3 Parent: Pay Rent 43

4 Senior: See Near 49

5 Cycles: Circles 57

6 Intimacy: In-To-Me-I-See 63

7 Relationships: Relation Ships 71

8 Enjoy: In Joy 83

9 Medication Or Meditation 89

10 Presents: Presence 95

11 Gratitude: Great Attitude 103

12 Pass Time: Pastime 115

13 SQ=IQ+EQ 121

14 Friend In Deed: Friend Indeed 127

15 It Is Not The End. It Is The Beginning. 137

About Manish Patel 141

1 *Inspiration*

"Do not think of it as cancer; it is gift from God, and I am going to enjoy every minute of it. I do not care what the doctors say. I am going to live more than 3 months - for sure."

Shreeraj's voice echoed through my mind constantly that day. I still thought of him as I headed to an appointment with one of my patients. I remember the way he sounded when he said it, like he was smiling through the phone even after being diagnosed with stage-three cancer in his right lung. Shreeraj had been all I could think about those past days. He was one of the best friends I have ever met.

On April 17th 2009, he left this world. We knew death was inevitable but he was trying to postpone it with his tremendous willpower. He told us of his sickness – his "gift" – as soon as the doctors found the aggressive tumor in his lung. He believed that he had received a gift from God in the form of cancer, and we were all silly to think it was a terrible thing.

Unlike most people, Shreeraj could not find problems when everyone else saw a problem. Knowing Shreeraj's positive outlook on life, I was not completely surprised that he thought of cancer as a gift.

Shreeraj was the type of person who could change the way people look at the world, with a simple conversation. He was exactly the kind of person that the world needed.

I wondered why it had to happen to him. This was a man who had touched every person he came into contact with, in a way that is difficult to explain. The world needed more people like him to inspire others to be happy no matter what. He had a quick smile and a massive heart, rivaled only by the size of his biceps. He was kind to everyone, quick to laugh, and as smart as a whip. To me, he was all-around perfect. It was impossible to dislike him. He made me feel at ease the moment he smiled.

Once Shreeraj passed away from us, I felt compelled to share the things he taught me with the rest of the world. But how would I do that?

I recall telling him to visit Michigan so that I could take him on popular shows to let people know the secret of his happiness even in the worst phase of life. At the time, I knew it was a joke, but now the joke is turning into reality as I tell the world about his philosophy through the legacy of Second Childhood.

I parked my car and focused on my next appointment. I put my grief aside and remembered to smile with Marie. I always enjoyed seeing her. She had a very friendly face and voice.

Marie never complained, even at the age of

98. Marie was lovely company. I walked through the door with a smile, and then I suddenly stopped in my tracks. I had walked in on Marie as her daughter helped her to change her diaper. I felt terrible; she was the last person I ever wanted to feel humiliated.

She laughed and shrugged when she saw me blushing.

"Sorry," I said awkwardly.

"It's okay, really. It's natural. When you've got to go, you've got to go".

While looking at Marie and her daughter, I thought of the old saying, "once a man and twice a child". I realized that this was Marie's second childhood and that her daughter had become her parent, at some point.

Marie gracefully embraced her old age and everything nature brings with it. She did not try to hide what was happening to her; she accepted it. I knew her to be a rational and happy person, and I was always very amazed and impressed by her. I thought about how I would have felt in her shoes. I would have been angry and embarrassed. I looked at her and then her daughter. She smiled at me. They both appeared happy. They seemed to have a great relationship. Marie's daughter was doing a great job of taking care of her.

I mentioned the second childhood concept

to them, during my visit. Both of them agreed with me about the importance of getting conversation going on the topic.

Marie looked happy, as any parent would be to have a child around. Marie accepted her daughter as her parent, with elegance. I thought about how it was great to see an adult child helping her aging parent. If we embraced old age and expected it to happen one day, it would not be so bad. Right? It might be God's way of forcing children to take care of their parents, to repay them for everything they have done for children. Marie was also setting a wonderful example for her children, and it was evident in the way her children treated her. It was beautiful.

Shreeraj crept back into my mind, with his amazingly positive view on everything in spite of any circumstances. I wished that I could introduce Marie to Shreeraj. The two are among the most beautiful, positive people I have met. It's sad that they will never have a chance to meet each other.

I thought of the first time I met Shreeraj, and smiled at how it almost did not happen. I was 20 years old, attending engineering school. My father wanted me to be a doctor, like himself, but I wanted nothing to do with it. He insisted that I give the profession a try. He believed vocation, whether by engineers, or doctors, was essential. But, he believed doctors had an advantage over engineers because they interacted with the people to help them face-to-face. Dad believed that working with people in-person helped to build relationships and receive blessings.

Dad tried to get me to study to become a Physical Therapist since I did not want to be a doctor. I agreed to join the healthcare profession because I liked his concept of earning blessings.

He took care of the paperwork, enrolled me in school, told me I could come back if I did not enjoy myself, and he even offered to send me to school in South India via plane. How could I say no to this? He gave me an introduction letter, to be delivered to a man who was attending the school.

I was extremely nervous; I was going to be really far away from the only friends and family I knew, to be in a place where I knew no one. I hoped this introduction letter found me some friends, fast.

When I entered the dorm, I walked to the register, mentioning that I had a letter for someone and was hoping to see him. Just as I finished my registration, a big man with an even bigger smile greeted me.

"Manish?"

"Shreeraj?"

"Yes, hello! How was your flight down?"

"Well, it was my first and it was amazing."

"Ok. Let's get your things upstairs."

"Wait, I have not been assigned to a room."

"It's no big deal. You can be one of my roommates, it's not like you know anybody here!"

I looked at this man in amazement and I quickly thanked God. He was right; I did not know anybody at school. I preferred to live with him to some stranger the desk would have assigned me. He was able to carry my entire load of luggage, and I stared at his back, trying to keep up while he laughed and joked all the way to his apartment.

We became fast friends. He was the most likeable person I had met, and I never stopped thanking God for my great luck in finding a friend like him. Even after I moved to North America, we kept in close contact. He was one of my best friends and I spoke with him regularly.

Learning of Shreeraj's diagnosis and death was the worst news I received in my life. When he was alive, he felt people who loved him should not be sad for his death. But, all of us were feeling his great loss.

I could not stop thinking about him as drove home. Traffic was bad. I was not going to be home anytime soon, and thoughts of my friend saddened me. I wished I were home to find comfort in my children and wife. Since that was not possible, I thought about Marie's diaper and walker.

I had learned a great deal from Marie in one afternoon. I had always known that my parents would age and I would eventually take care of them. But until recently, I saw this as something I would do out of duty rather than something that could be beautiful. I thought of the duty towards my children, that I was responsible for them. But, the fact that I loved them made the duty fun and welcome. I imagined that I could approach taking care of my parents the same way I took care of my children, and it would benefit us all.

I love my parents very dearly. If we could approach the aging process as something natural that we could all enjoy, it would make life easier. I would smile at them like Shreeraj smiled at me when we first met. I would care for them like Shreeraj cared for everyone, and in the same way Marie and her daughter had shown me.

I thought about how much easier the lives of seniors would be if their children cared for them. There had to be a way to get this message out. I thought of all the parental magazines I had read in doctors' waiting rooms but I could not find anything on the subject of parenting a parent.

That evening, on my way back to home, I decided to write a book about second childhood. I began to discuss this concept with my patients and started recording their results, along with my thoughts, on the subject.

With Second Childhood, it is my hope that we show parents that dependency is not curse; it is a blessing. We must prepare to parent our parents and to bring beauty to their second childhood. Whether we are changing their diapers, helping them with their walkers and wheelchairs, or simply having a conversation, we can show them respect, love and affection.

Just as a child does not mind if mom changes his or her diaper, aging parents should not mind if their adult children have to change their diapers. Second Childhood encourages everyone to help his or her aging parents have a graceful, respectful, and loving second childhood.

Live for someone else, even if for a brief period. When we do, the sensation is wonderful. It makes us feel closer to life. And remember, we will also face a second childhood, should we be blessed to live long enough. Our kids are watching us. We can expect the same respect and love from our kids that we give to our parents.

2 Question: Quest on

In June of 2010, I was going through a really tough time. My personal life felt very difficult after a nearly tragic incident in February 2010, which I describe later. My wife suffered from Post Traumatic Stress Disorder. And, I did not work on my book, for some time.

One day, while returning from an afternoon meeting, I drove through the downtown area to reach home. I saw a beautiful park close to the river so I decided take a break here to avoid downtown traffic. I parked my car and took my notebook to the park. My notebook had no entries for a long time.

The water was shimmering with sunlight. It seemed like the perfect day in this little space of land so I decided to try to center myself at the park. I looked around for a bit, before I started writing. Everything seemed perfect today. People strolled and they held hands. Healthy grass was everywhere. Children laughed and played.

I saw seniors walking by, which brought joy in my heart. I let everything flood over me and I immediately felt peaceful and happier. I opened my notebook and began to write about joy.

My head was down in the notebook when I heard someone call for my attention. I looked up to face two seniors. One of them said, "Young man, people usually come to this park to enjoy. So, why did you bring your homework here?"

I was taken by her question, because she had broken my focus while I was "in the zone". I thought for a moment and then I looked her in the eye and said, "I am doing this homework for you honey. I'm writing a book to prepare a better parent for your second childhood."

She asked what a second childhood was, so I told her about my plans for this book. She was so intrigued at the idea that I watched her entire demeanor change.

At the end of our conversation she stared at me for a second with a smile on her face, and then she said, "Son, would you give me a free hug?"

I replied to her, "yes", right away and that day, I became the richest person on earth. I still feel that hug everyday and think about her.

I was just a stranger on a bench in some park, but she felt moved enough to hug me. Over the course of our conversation, she went from referring to me as 'young man', to 'Son'. This struck me and I became more certain about writing this book.

She solidified my belief in the importance of reaching out to people with the second childhood concept. She even took my business card and told me she would put it in a picture frame until she found my picture on my book; and then she would replace the business card with my picture.

That lady in the park helped me to grow more confident. I began to speak to more people about the concept of second childhood. Everyone believed that I was doing something necessary for a higher purpose.

That is how one question became a quest for me. I bought a voice recorder the next day and started recording for Second Childhood in my car.

SECOND CHILDHOOD | 42 | Manish Patel

3 Parent: Pay Rent

SECOND CHILDHOOD | 44 | Manish Patel

I was driving from my home to my office, on one of the most beautiful sunny days. At the time, I was so busy with my work and family life that I did not make time to write, even though my mind was full of thoughts about Second Childhood. Instead of trying to find time to write, I decided to record my thoughts while driving.

While driving that day, I discovered the true meaning of the word, 'parent'. I heard a whisper from, and was thankful to, God on this special day. I started my recorder to take notes for this chapter.

I learned the true meaning of word parent symbolized our duty to 'pay rent'. We never forget to pay rent for our house, office or other services, so how can we forget to pay the most important rent to our parents? Like other collection agencies, God is the highest special collection agency. Rent can be paid in the form of respect and love.

As children, we have infinite expectations from our parents. Our parents are usually our first memories. They shower us with love and affection. We often have a hard time growing out of this as we age. Sometimes, we become so self-centered that we expect to be pampered, in some ways, for the rest of our living days.

As adults, we often forget that our parents hope to be treated the same, in old age, as they treated us when we were growing up. We have to remember that our parents' excellent years were spent tending to us. We have to remind ourselves that our relationship with them has not ended just because we no longer need their assistance to stand on our own.

We cannot ignore the fact that our parents' investments in us, with money they worked hard for, were in our best interests. When our parents were young, they spent every dime on us. They plan retirements to make sure they are as little burden as possible on children. The fact that they tie their futures to our welfare and best interest shows their love and concern for us.

In the words of a book, there is no way to do justice to all a parent does for a child. Their deeds are without equal; a price tag cannot be put on everything they are, and have been to us.

Until we become parents, we cannot totally understand what it is like for someone to be fully dependent on us. As parents, do we ever stop to think what it took for our parents to do this? Most of us have not. Respect everything our parents did to ensure we faced as few hardships as possible.

Our parents deceived us continually during young years. They led us to believe parenting was easy. They did this for us because they love us. They think of us as the best things to ever happen to them, no matter what we have done.

We must think of their situations in order to

properly analyze what they did and why they did it. Often, upon reflection, we will find respect for their intellect and efficiency. They used to worry about us to no end as they did an immense number of things for us. Once we realize these truths, and understand their meanings, we will know that no matter what we do for them, we will never give back the undying love we received.

We need to ask ourselves, what is next? Reading about something is not the same as *doing* something. Good intentions without action are never enough. The ideas read wonderfully on paper, like instructions to assemble a piece of furniture. It is not until we begin to put the parts together that we realize the process is difficult.

In order to achieve selflessness that we strive for, we must rewind back to the days when we were children. We have to find tools to help us realize true love, respect and admiration for our parents. It's only then that our actions and work are genuine. We must resurface feelings buried deep within the bottomless pit of wants and needs so we can find what is needed to help our parents through their second childhood.

Just as my friend Shreeraj loved every one, even in the worst phase of his life, God wants us to pay rent by showing love and respect to our parents. This love we direct to our parents is an indirect way of worshiping God. In spiritual terms,

God is our ultimate parent and birth is considered gift of God. Our parents are the reason for our existence as they serve as the shell to nurture us until we are ready to meet the world through birth. It is their love that gives us life.

If we try to love our parents with respect, it has added value. Remember this:

>**R**everence
>
>**E**mpathy
>
>**S**acrifices
>
>**P**assion
>
>**E**motion
>
>**C**are
>
>**T**hanks

By showing our respect and thanks to our parents, we are showing our respect and thanks to God. We have been granted a golden chance to take care of them, to act as parents to our parents in their second childhood.

When our parents get their second set of walker and diapers in their second childhood, we must accept our roles as parents for our parents. We should not blow the chance to love them; once they are gone, it's too late to pay rent.

4 Senior: See Near

Once I understood the true meaning of the word parent, I started thinking about the word 'senior'. I knew, for sure, that God must have kept some secret in this word, as well. I thought a lot about it, but I could not find a hidden secret in the word 'senior'.

During my monthly meeting with my staff of 24 physical therapists, I try to teach them how to develop intimacy with patients. In my ten-year career as a physical therapist, I found intimacy is the best way to promote faster healing in patients.

At another one of my monthly meetings, I talked with them about how to develop nearness with patients. All of a sudden, I realized that I had found the secret behind the word 'senior'.

The word symbolizes, 'see near'. I thanked God, again, for revealing a secret of a word. As a result of this discovery, I told my therapists to see their patients as near to their hearts. When our parents enter their second childhoods, we should keep them near and dear to us.

A role reversal occurs, as children become parents to their parents while parents become children to their children. Do not consider your parents life transition to second childhood merely in the sense of needing a caretaker. We must remember that our parents did their best to offer us happiness in our dependent years.

For many of us, childhood was a carefree time, filled with laughter and joy. We should do what we can to fill our parents' lives with this same happiness and enjoyment.

A wheelchair, often considered a necessary component of old age, is similar to the stroller. We use diapers as children, and the same diapers come back to us when we enter old age. There is a sense of need and vulnerability in each stage, leading to the need for a caretaker.

The concept of childhood should be a fine thought where love and happiness are unbound and unlimited. Quite often though, our parents are not enjoying their second childhood. Often, their adult children have families of their own, and being a 24-hour caretaker just does not seem possible. That does not mean that we cannot give parents what we had. We do not have to take the 'all or nothing' approach to caring for and respecting our parents during their aging.

Think of the love and attention showered upon you when you were a child. Think of how secure you felt knowing that no matter what, you could rely on your parents. You must do your best to provide your parents with the unquestioned love you were privileged to receive from them when you were young.

Despite the fact that most of us will never forget what our parents once did for us, we often come to a standstill in our affairs with them. At times, these pauses in relationships are because we are too busy to do what is right. Life can be hectic, and today's world is much busier than the one our parents experienced when they were younger. It is difficult for us to have enough time for ourselves. Often, the reason for a standstill is traced to differences in opinion. Sometimes, our parents make choices they feel are in the best interests of us, but we do not always agree with their decisions. These differences often lead to a downslide when no common ground can be found.

Even if we do not always agree with our parents, we should not deliberately let this affect relationship with one another. I often wished, after such a debate, that my father would think as I do about whatever was creating the rift between us. It's not always possible to agree. Part of maturing is learning how to find common ground and get along with people when we do not agree with their thoughts or actions – our parents especially.

Compromise is critical in relationships. Be truthful and genuine, and also meditate on the differences between you and your parents. Find out your differences and analyze them to work to resolve them. Improving the relationship with a parent can be a gradual activity. You may not see results immediately, but you must keep working on a relationship to keep it healthy and evolving.

There comes a point where we realize all of life is a stage. We have heard the saying before; it's true. Actors cannot always tell how well they are playing a role when they are on stage. It might be difficult to see one's faults and weaknesses firsthand. Directors, producers, and other actors critique them, and they look back on performances at a later time.

Life is similar to this. Sometimes, we do not learn what we are doing wrong until someone near to us, who cares for our performance, points it out. Often, the ones with the least selfish intentions are our parents. They're often the most honest and the most invested in our life because they want us to do well. Many times they are advising us on things they have learned firsthand. They have lived longer than us, experienced more life, made more mistakes, and learned more lessons.

Just because our parents are getting older, it does not mean their advice is outdated. They will advise us most honestly and with sincerity. Just because we are in a position to also give advice does not mean we outgrow the need for our parents to be part of our life. It's up to us to make the relationship reciprocal in nature.

Many of us focus on all of the things that we need to do in our lives, and as a result, we often neglect our parents' needs and advice, thinking we know better. We fail to see what is near and dear to us while we are self-sustaining, possibly even thriving. We have to remember that we're in this position for a reason. We are lucky to have been shaped into the people that we are today. Often, our most pivotal shapers are our parents, which should be reason enough to consider their advice and pay attention to them.

From time to time, we feel nagged by our parents, and rightfully so. They can be pushy, and forceful. These ego clashes seem to increase as we age. Parents must keep in mind that children have expectations, desires, dreams, and hopes of their own. Because their children's dreams may not align with their own that does not mean their children are wide of the mark.

Children and parents, both, need to find a common ground. It's all part of growing up. Just because we do not get taller does not mean we are done growing. Our hearts and minds should expand faster than our waistlines. Open your heart to everything, including your parents. *See* what is *nearest* to you, who made your life possible.

5 Cycles: Circles

A person's life is divided into three phases: childhood, adulthood, and old age. We cannot change this order; it is a law of nature. While we cannot change the order, we can choose to enjoy each phase.

Life starts with being children. We grow up, learning about the world and ourselves. Many of us get married, bring new life to earth, and then we enter old age where we become children again while our children become our parents. What an interesting cycle of circles!

When we were small children, our parents dropped us at daycare centers while they went to work. When parents grow old, many of their adult children get too busy with work, so they leave their parents at adult daycare centers. Many of the things parents do for their children, when they are infants and dependent, are done for parents once they age and become dependent.

Visiting an adult daycare center, one might wonder if the residents really were once young and energetic. It is unbelievable how our bodies decline due to aging. Someday, we will become part of the cycle, at daycares, feeble, and in need of help to eat and change clothes.

Life is full of enormous surprises and the peculiarity of life can be with nothing. If you have missed certain parts of your life cycles and circles, revisit them to repair any damage. Long periods away from loved ones reduce the size of circles. Do not forget about people in your circle; stay connected with them.

If we fall short of interaction within a circle, we no longer are part of a circle. At some point, without attention, our circles and cycles are broken and compromised. Let's not reach a point where we have to say, "If only I gave a little more effort, if only I tried harder, things would have been better. If only I paid more attention when I needed to...."

With gradual passage of time, love often fades in relationships. It is up to us to keep love alive by expressing it at the forefront of our lives. We must work to reduce the number of times we take love ones for granted.

Every effort to love will give us so much. If our parents can take such care of us, and provide us with so much love and security, why should it be difficult for us to take on the sacred duty to look after them in their second childhood?

If you have not spoken to your parent for some time due to a prideful standstill, put the pride to the side. If you have not spoken to your parent because you are busy, then adjust your calendar to make your parents a part of your schedule. Get in touch. Do not wait because before you know it, all of our parents will be at their final standstill, eternally out of reach.

Recently, I called my dear friend Shreeraj's wife to make sure everything was going well. She asked me about this book's progress. We talked about Shreeraj and his influence on this book. We spoke of his many great qualities, and we spent time catching up on things.

I thought about Shreeraj's parents and the great influence they had within his life. I thought of how much Shreeraj loved his parents. He never hesitated to go to them for support, or provide them with whatever they needed in life.

Shreeraj loved his parents as much as they loved him. He believed in harmony between all people. He also believed that love started at home and branched out to the rest of humanity.

We would talk about the dismantling of the family in many of today's cultures, and how adult children did not seem to have time for their aging parents. As parents slowed down from natural aging, children sped past them, busy with their own life activities. Parents were aging to a point where they required help, just as a child needs help, and many seniors were without a support system. Shreeraj and I would talk about this and many things that hinder, or improve, a person's way of life and our world.

Shreeraj and I believe that everyone should start living for their parents as they enter second childhood. Start doing great things for them to make them feel your love. Even with all we might think we are doing for them, it might not be much compared to what they have done for us. Our love and adoration for them should increase as time passes, through all of life's cycles and circles.

6 Intimacy: In-To-Me-I-See

SECOND CHILDHOOD | 64 | Manish Patel

If we take a deep, philosophical look into the word intimacy, we can break it down as 'Into-me-I-see'. To have intimacy with God means we are doing our best to see God within ourselves. Having intimacy with another person means we are trying to see bits of God and ourselves within that person. The more of ourselves we see in people, the deeper spiritual connection we have with them because of our intimate understanding of who they are as people.

Intimacy allows insight into thoughts and habits as we share them with another. It's when we start seeing God in others, and within, that our relationships are divine.

We agree that as we age and get wrapped up in our lives, our parents often take a backseat. We forget about the connection between them and us. Deliberately or not, we disregard them so we can have more time for other things. Partially because of their unconditional love for us, we take this love for granted. Often times, it is laziness that leads to disregard.

Additionally, we sometimes find our work problems trumping our personal ones. We go to work early, stay at work late, work through most of the weekend, and bring work at home - just to feel like we are on top of all of our endless obligations and responsibilities.

Even though we need to earn money to pay bills, we cannot assign monetary value to our relationships with friends or family, especially the priceless one we have with our parents.

We might also experience torment, anxiety or other things that prevent us from improving relationships with people nearest to us. Often times, it is fear at the root of our obstacles. We do not repair things with our loved ones because we are afraid of our reactions or feelings. We fear confronting our failings. So instead, we do nothing. It is okay to realize you are not perfect. Nobody is perfect. We are to learn from our shortcomings and imperfections.

Despite conveniences of today's high-tech communication, gadgets and computers tend to put added strain on relationships. For example, a father and son might share a weak link by sharing text messages instead of sharing voices. A brother may spend more time with his mobile phone than siblings. A daughter can drift away from a mother, as she is drawn into social networking tools.

Regardless of how advanced we get, with conveniences never imaginable 20 years ago, we seem to become lazier, more confined to ease, and eventually separated from our loved ones. If we are not careful, technical advances will prevent us from real connections with people. Do not get me wrong; I completely support advancement and evolution. But, people need to use tools in smarter ways so they do not divide us from our circles.

Times may have changed since our parents were our age, but one thing has not: sacrifices are still necessary in every relationship. This includes sacrificing pride when you should admit that you are wrong. There is more to lose when you do not admit your faults. Show gratitude for relationships. Nurture them. Keep them alive.

I know that we cannot expect the world to change at once; there is no chance of change if change does not start somewhere. Charity begins at home; change does too. We can initiate change by making a list of our fears and problems. Next, sort these fears and problems out, and then repair the damaged breaks. You might reflect on your relationship with God or a higher power that you call upon. Or, you can meditate with the universe, thinking about all of your life's experiences.

Change should start within our families. It strengthens relations between friends. It is also a wonderful visual example for children. Our children will likely become parents, some day. They should have the privilege to witness the love we show our parents, and it is a great model for them to follow.

If we want good children, we have to start by being good mothers and fathers. We have got to improve before we can expect any improvement outside of us.

Minds work similar to flashlights. We shine light on certain parts of our minds and realities, while other parts are left to darkness. We forget about the pain we caused to others, and instead focus on the pain that others have caused to us. Think about some of your important relationships. Often, we remember bad times, and focus on mistakes while forgetting about good times.

We need to work on moving beyond bad instances and learn to embrace good ones. We have to focus on optimism to help us become stronger in our resolve to be great people, and redefine our character.

The type of relationship that we have with our parents depends on our mindset; so changing our outlook to a positive one is a step forward. Fixing broken relationships requires fixing broken links within. We must constantly seek ways to improve ourselves so we can mentally, physically, and spiritually forge healthy relations.

Imagine if we all put brakes on laziness, and stepped it up a notch to improve? We would not only improve our lives but we could improve the lives of others. If we came a little closer to reach our fullest potential as humans, we would find ourselves living in a different world.

If our relationship with our parents suffers, we lose intimacy. We have to learn how to open our minds and see bits of our parents within us, and see bits of ourselves within them. They are a gift from the universe, to love us and forgive us unconditionally. They are the ones who will gift us the insight that we need to become our best.

I know it is tough to break habits and adapt to change, especially in mindset, but it will prove worthwhile. Change your outlook; communicate. Do not wait until your parents have died to tell them what you feel. Tell them now. A relationship cannot be repaired once we pass from this life. We must work to have no regrets when it comes to the love we show our parents and spouses.

It is time to explore this word 'intimacy' and try to develop it with our loved ones. Once we close our eyes, we should be able to see our loved ones within us. If we find success doing so, then we can use the word 'intimacy' to characterize our relationship with them.

7 Relationships: Relation Ships

Each morning when I wake up, I turn my head to the right and begin to mentally map out my day. One of the first things I see is a gold plated teacup and saucer. This tea set serves a huge purpose in my life. Every morning, the cup and saucer silently remind me that this is a day where I will not just be working and "doing my job". Each day, I will work to do my part to serve elders and those around me. I must make it a mission to create strong relationships with people and do my part to leave the world a better place than I found.

The word 'relationship' has deep meaning. "Ships" take goods from one place to another. A relationship takes our inner goods, love, emotions and thoughts, into another person while bringing their goods into us. Relationships are reciprocal, based on giving through love and sharing thoughts with another.

As we regularly interact with people, it is inevitable that we build a connection with them. It is through relationships that we can exchange love and emotions into each other.

When we stop to reflect upon all the people in our lives and our connections with them, we better understand ourselves, and those around us. With understanding, we can realize the things God meant for us to realize: high regards for humanity, respect for moral values, and gratitude for all we are given.

Thinking of relationships as an inner goods exchange system changed my life and the life of one of my patients. The first time I met Lucille was a Tuesday in April 2005. She was 99 years old and living in her own apartment at an assisted-living facility.

She had been unable to walk for the last two and a half years. Usually therapists meet with patients for six to eight weeks, depending on their needs and response to therapy. The treatment period can obviously be extended. In Lucille's case, her need was great, as was her response to therapy, so I extended her treatment. In two and one half months, she went from being completely bedridden to being able to walk at least 100 feet at a time.

I believe her recovery sped up because I had been able to treat her mind by developing a rapport with her. It was through our friendship that I was able to share in her excitement to get to the dining area without a wheelchair. Just ten weeks into her therapy, she had found happiness and excitement in her achievements; and I was lucky to witness her joys and to share them with her.

One Tuesday afternoon, I noticed her eyes appeared more red than usual. I told her to make an appointment with an ophthalmologist for as soon as possible. After more thought, we decided it would be best if I called her doctor to set it up.

She was lucky to get an appointment for the next day. Her goddaughter agreed to drive her.

Thursday, I saw Lucille for our regular visit, hoping that she was doing fine after visiting the ophthalmologist. Instead, Lucille's whole eye had turned red. When I stepped close to her, I saw the whites of her eyes were invisible.

"What happened? What did the doctor say yesterday, Lucille?"

"Actually, I was not able to go to my appointment yesterday."

"Why not?"

"My goddaughter did not show up, so I missed my appointment."

I realized that if I did not take her she might not go at all. I called her doctor to explain the situation. He said he could take us right away, so I cleared the rest of my afternoon.

Lucille used her walker to get to the front door, and then I carried her to my car. It was a beautiful moment. She was so small and frail that it was like lifting a child. Looking back, I am able to connect that moment to the concept behind this book. And, I also understood the role of second parenthood, as I held her as I would my child. She held onto me like a child holds a parent, carefully and with faith that nothing will happen to her.

The ophthalmologist told us Lucile arrived just in time to save her eyesight. That moment was so beautiful, the moment I found out that I was able to do something for Lucille to be okay for another day.

On our drive home, Lucille and I got into a conversation about her life. I did not know much about her personal life, as I never wanted to pry. I shared information about my wife and son, and I would regularly show her pictures of my son.

On our drive home, she knew we would be passing my house. She asked me to call my wife so she could meet her and also hold my young son who was only a month old at the time.

Lucille was too tired to get out of the car, when we arrived at my home, so my wife brought my son to the driveway. My wife and Lucille spoke for a bit as Lucille held my son. Before we left, she spent a few minutes smiling and gazing at him. She asked my wife to come to visit with her prince. We laughed a bit and then headed on.

During our drive to Lucille's home, she was quiet for a bit. And then she said, "Manish I want to share something with you. I am the widow of a successful doctor. I have a lot of money and property and, I really have nobody to share it with. All of my things will go to various charities and my goddaughter, the same goddaughter that could not take me to my doctor's appointment. It was you who stood by me. I would like to write my will so that you will receive everything."

I was floored by her proposal. I had no idea what to say. I started by thanking her and denying her offer. There is no way I could accept such a thing. My rejection was not because we were not blood-related. I appreciated her feelings, proposal and her love for me. It just did not feel right to take anything in return for building a nice relationship with her. I tried to explain my reasoning to her - it did not feel ethical on a personal level. Lucille then suggested rewriting her will, so my son would be the benefactor.

I told her this; "God has a plan for me. If I have worked hard enough to deserve that kind of wealth, He will find a way to get it to me. I know this is not the way. I just want your well wishes and love."

I had no desire to take things in return for building strong relationships with my patients. If I did, I would not have taken the time to know them. I would just learn enough about them to take from them and give little in return. This is not my nature, neither is it something I was taught by my parents.

My father taught me the importance of good relationships so we can receive blessings and personal fulfillment from our work while seeing real changes in people's well being. This changed the way I approach all personal relationships.

It was after this conversation, with my dad, that I accepted the gold plated teacup and saucer from Lucile. It was her way of showing gratitude to me, and her appreciation for our friendship. I look at it every morning, and think about everything I learned from her. I remind myself to continue life, giving from my bottomless heart, knowing the less we focus on what we can receive from a person, the more we can grow as a person. I chose not to accept money for expressing love, and I have no regrets. Sure, money is good, but love is greater.

Unfortunately, too often, people will obsess over money and trade their souls for it. If it is not money, it can be obsession with material things. Think of relationships, and portions of ourselves, that we sacrifice to amass more stuff. There is more to life than material accumulation.

We ride around on material ships that sink from their own weight, as we watch relationships sail by. We need to re-evaluate our priorities. We must sail on relationships, not material ships.

While money is a sure means to material, we cannot blame money for material obsession. In itself, money is not evil. It's our obsession with money that is destructive to us. Remember, there is more to life than material items and money.

The more I write of my life with my patients, friends and family, the more I realize the happiest times in my life were the times spent with loved ones. Whether it is enduring through tough times together, laughing, or simply being together, those moments are invaluable.

We decide what we value. Nobody should be able to tell us what is to be and what is not to be valued. Now, do not get me wrong. I have a company. I earn money. I love providing money for my family, and I love that I will (God willing) be able to pay my children's college tuition. And yes, providing money for my family does require me to work long hours at times, but I know when it is time to put work on hold.

For those of us who let our work trump our personal lives, we must learn to strike a healthy balance between the two facets. If work consumes the majority of our time, we may have to consider reducing our workloads. We might earn less, but we will begin to depend more on relationships than material. And, we will realize that we will not need as much. We will be wealthier from our personal affairs than we could ever be with material things.

To offset money we lose by working lesser hours, make fewer purchases. As we change our lifestyle, we can save almost $1,200 per year just by making coffee at home rather than stopping at coffee shops. All the money saving lessons that our mothers taught us really work. When we look closely, we will see there are often more practical ways to live our lives.

Again, we choose all the things we value. Our relationships should be valuable to us: our friends, family, and of course, parents. Little is as fulfilling as being a hero to our parents in their second childhood.

While I was working on this book, someone asked me if I was going to include my family tree. He said he hoped my family tree looked better than the trees outside. I looked outside. It was a typical Michigan winter day with naked, frozen trees surrounding me. There is something so sad and deathly about a leafless tree.

Thinking of the family tree, I considered the leaves that bring life and beauty to the trees. They are similar to relationships in life, and they are the most beautiful part of life. Relationships provide nourishment to grow family trees.

When leaves fall off a tree, they float away with a sense of loveliness and happiness. But in reality, as beautiful as this looks to us, once a leaf descends from a tree, it is dead. In the same way, when we float too far away from our family tree, collapse feels imminent.

For many adults, the first parenthood can be tough and overwhelming. We raise our children with no experience, even if we have help. When we begin to care for our aging parents, we must draw from the experiences of our 'first parenthood' to find love and patience to deal with issues.

When we care for our aging parents, we find ourselves in the same ship we were in during our first parenthood. Just as we were with our children, we are often afraid of what our parents are going to do; what they cannot do; and if they will get hurt.

Instead of ignoring our parents and seeing them as nuisances, we should encourage them to accept our tender, loving care. If you have children at home, involve them in respecting, loving, and caring for their grandparents. Our kids benefit from relationships with our parents; grandparents give grandchildren the world they often could not give to their children. As we age and enter our second childhood, our children will have seen the beauty that can come with taking care of parents.

When the time comes to help our parents, we must not leave them out to dry. Be careful not to neglect them for money and material. Money and material did not raise us from naïve infants into strong adults; our parents did that.

Most of us have had to make due without money and we managed to survive, often because we had friends and family to help get us through difficult times. Money is great but it cannot hug or love you. What's a world without love? Empty. Sail on relationships and watch money, success, and happiness fall into place.

8 Enjoy: In Joy

Just like people who are not in the spotlight, famous historical figures also endured hardships. Some grew up very poor while some grew up with a lot of opportunity. Most of them did not receive a memo stating, "Here it is. Here's the moment you need to seize to change the world."

Instead, many of them started on a mission, committed to it, and saw it through. Commitment requires great change for some of us. And like any other obligation, it comes with responsibility. We need to stop making excuses. We need to stop saying things like, "That's the way I am. I cannot help it." Throwing a weak excuse into the universe does not pardon us of anything. It does not free us of responsibility. We have a duty to commit to a cause greater than us; it is our purpose.

Some of us have lived through awful events that have disheartened us. While some of these events were uncontrollable, it is how we respond to these situations that is in our control. The best way to react to a negative is to change it into a positive. We become what we are, as the result of our actions and decisions. The lack of a sense of responsibility does not erase it.

Inner happiness is neither bought nor found outside of us. Only by feeling grateful can we be happy. We have to be grateful for all that we have been given, the good and bad times. These times shape us into the people we are to become.

It is said, "The happiest of men are not those who have a lot, but those who are able to give much because they require little." I read this on a sign in a coffee shop while working on this book. The happiest people are in joy most of the time because they fully enjoy all of life's offerings. They see brilliance in everything around them.

Most of us have seen beauty with the birth of our kids, nieces and nephews, and children of our dearest friends. We witness the amazingly joyous miracle that is our existence by seeing it in another. We see that life is most beautiful in the moments with family, when we experience love and recognize connections that we have with other human beings. If we think of all relationships as beautiful, and a serious responsibility, we will want to be a part of loving circles. Meditating on life's beauty and relationships can provide a renewed sense of purpose to be there for your parents.

If our parents are no longer with us, we are not free from responsibility to a higher purpose. We can visit and spend time with people who do not have families. These gestures bring joy and mean so much to the people whom we visit. This kindness leads to significant self-development. We attain greatness with noble duty and aspiration to do our best. Do your best; you will find joy.

Happiness, just like character, lies beneath the skin. Within each of us is equal great power.

We are all the same. Once we realize this, we can realize one way to find happiness and greatness is through a dedication to do better.

Dedication to change and to a higher cause can be tiring. It can be draining to stay committed, even though we know we are bringing happiness to another human being. It can be difficult to stay positive. But, just like everything else in life, we have to work at it. Do not be impatient if things do not go perfectly as soon as you execute a plan or extend a loving hand to another person. Do not give up. You'll see results, and you will find joy in the outcome.

A visionary, my dear friend, Shreeraj stayed positive through everything that happened in life, including his battle with illness. He never became impatient with people and he never gave up on life and relationships. He believed that we must get up and walk after a fall. He managed to keep a smile on his face at all times, even when those around him were crying at the very thought of losing him.

We lost Shreeraj at the tender age of 34. He will never be forgotten. His legacy carries on through many who were blessed to share in his contagious love for life. Even though he smiled freely and loved life, Shreeraj by no means took easy routes. He worked hard to leave a positive mark on this world. While his quest was often difficult, Shreeraj stayed focused on his purpose to spread love to all, knowing his compassionate heart would help to make the world a better place, one person at a time.

It takes courage and selflessness to stand by our friends and parents when they need us. It takes compassion, empathy, and strength to stand with them in times of need. Our parents need us to realize our duty to them.

Strength and commitment to relationships has preserved humanity throughout the ages. By realizing that we are fundamentally the same, we will feel more compassion for other people.

Take a breath be happy. Enjoy being in joy.

9 Medication Or Meditation

During a visit to Canada, I met one of my college friends whom I had not seen in 10 years. I could not believe the positive change I saw in him. He explained the key role that meditation played in his life. Through meditation, he had found peace, using the same practices as yogis.

Ancient yogis lived in jungles, to find peace using meditation. Many of us cannot leave a fast life and go to the jungle, but we can find peace and happiness. While medical technology can take care of our physical health, it cannot improve our mental and spiritual health.

Today, many people are walking around with the day-to-day stress of meeting work and personal obligations. Stress is a silent killer. Stress can widen distance between loved ones and it can destroy relationships. Meditation is one of the best ways to eliminate stress.

The word yoga, derived from the word *yuj*, means to have control or to unite. Yogis meditate to develop sensory control. They reach a high spiritual level in spite of being a part of the world, as we know it. It may be surprising to know many yogis lived over 100 years. And, they achieved this longevity without any medication; they practiced meditation. Yogis lead holistic lives, drawing on sciences to improve life. They connect knowledge and experience to a constantly improving mental, spiritual, and physical life cycle.

Many of us can never dream of living as long as yogis because of the way our bodies have become with time's passage. Today, it is difficult to survive under any normal conditions. But, yogis' trained bodies are suited for adverse conditions: hunger, pain, and isolation.

Yogis lived with an unbreakable bond to joy and happiness. They promoted life and peace, which kept poisonous stress out of the body. Yogis found pleasure from whatever they saw. For them, it was much easier to enjoy life because they enjoyed *everything* life offered. When we nurture environment, it nurtures us. There is a constant flow of positive energy that fills us. When we give out love, we often receive love in return.

Today, yoga's role in the medical industry has increased. Aware of yoga's benefit to mental, spiritual, and physical health, many experts now recommend it to enhance health. Yoga helps to remove worldly doting and strengthen connection to humankind. Yogis bring valuable lessons for us to learn, believing that everyone's help is needed to make our human cause a success story.

After talking with my college friend, I started meditating for 30 minutes every day. Since starting the practice, I see a great difference in my energy level. I knew of the concept for years, but I did not implement it into my life until I saw the positive difference in my friend's life.

My initial plan was to stay in Canada for two days, but I stayed for almost four days. I did not feel like coming back since I was learning some of the greatest lessons of life. Since that day, I find peace with the help of meditation. My friend also taught me about astral body travel and cosmic energy. We talked about how we absorb cosmic energy through meditation.

I fell in love with meditation because it is an ideal way to avoid medication. As noted by World Health Organization, health is a state of physical, mental, social, and spiritual being. The mind and body are interconnected.

Meditation connects the mind and body to the ultimate source of the universe. It is how we absorb cosmic energy.

Similarly, we all connect to our parents and loved ones through love, affection and emotions. When we connect to our parents on an improved level, we develop stronger bonds that improve the quality of their lives. And through meditation, we teach them how to improve their minds, bodies, and spirit, thereby adding increased peace and joy to their lives.

10 Presents: Presence

During youthful times, when we are most at risk, our parents are our security. They protect us when we are unable to protect ourselves. They are there when we wake each morning, with a roof overhead. Each night, they deliver the comfort a child needs to find rest.

As we grow from children into young adults, we continue to rely on our parents for just about everything: clothes, lunch money, school supplies, phones, haircuts, allowance, and on and on. Some parents are able to provide for their children, with no financial limit. But, many children would trade material things for quality time with parents. Our parents often feel the same way about us once they reach the stage of their second childhood. They would prefer that we visit, if just for an hour, instead of the impersonal Hallmark card.

As stated earlier, many of us overlook our parents' wishes and needs because we are on call for our careers, errands, and life pursuits. This is not to say that having and reaching goals is a bad thing. I urge you to improve yourself, but it is about balancing life's intricacies. It's okay to chase your dreams; but take time to partake in relationships.

Do we really need more things to be happy or do we want more so people will believe we are happy? Being happy is really about being. It is not about being or having one thing. Being ourselves and honest, we see happiness is already in us.

People think that they need more and, in turn, work hard long hours to provide more, while spending more time away from their families. We hire a cleaning staff, babysitters, nurses, home managers, and secretaries. All kinds of people make up for our absences at home just so we can work to invest in more stuff.

If people respect us based solely on the things we have, we are really not well respected. We must stop getting into uncertain situations, where material defines our status. Stop investing in objects, and start investing in relationships.

A short time ago, one of my friend's fathers passed away. The father worked extremely hard for most of his life. He was an engineer. He owned multiple properties; he invested heavily in stocks as well as hobbies.

As we cleaned out the father's condo, we packed a lot of stuff, and more clothes than I could own in a lifetime. His family has all this stuff now - stuff that they will never need or use, stuff that will never replace him.

His dad died twice divorced, leaving behind a strained relation with his middle child. I do not question his intelligence, his drive to succeed, and his desire to provide the best for his family. His achievements, when younger, afforded his family the ability to travel the world. But it did make me think about the choice some people make to chase materialistic presents and forget about the value of people presence.

During our friendship, I barely got to know my friend's father because he was convinced that he always needed more things. He would show his face at our school programs, but he was always late and left early. He took the obligatory pictures before he left, but he was never really present. His children really took note of his absence. Now he is gone forever.

Recently, I had a conversation about my friend's dad. I considered how much stuff I have bought over the last 5 or 10 years. The stuff did not really make me happy in the long run. Think of the fancy new things you have purchased after a bad breakup or a rough patch in life. The new things may have helped you feel better, but the feeling was fleeting.

Material did not make me happy because the majority of it is in my basement. My wallet got thick with receipts as I bought more stuff. Receipts showed money 'we used to have', now in the form of things collecting cobwebs. Receipts have no 'happiness' guarantee.

When I look back at my life, it was not new shoes that got me through tough times. It was the time I spent with my parents over dinner, finding myself through them. It was time with friends, building relationships. Love will always fill holes that possessions will not fill.

My friend cannot change his childhood with his absentee father. Today, this is still a sore spot for him. But, he is thankful for everything his father provided for him. The first step to healing was after his father became ill. My friend became the ideal son, working fewer hours, and standing at his father's side. He traded presents for presence.

Whatever your reasons for not being happy, share and express your concerns, and let them stay in the past. You cannot change the past. But you can change the way that you deal with it. We need to look for the opportunity in hardship.

Our parents were our first and, often, best teachers. By example and interaction with them, we learned basic survival skills. It's still the same today; older relatives can teach us things to help us lead better lives. Instead of ignoring them, we would be wise to listen to all of their stories and learn from their mistakes.

Once, after a lecture at an assisted-living facility, a caregiver asked me how could parents expect presence if they never offered presence? She said her dad was an alcoholic and her mom could not care for 7 kids. She told me that she never received the love and care that she felt that she needed during her childhood.

I told her to remember what Jesus said, to

forgive people because they do not know what they do. In the end, the root of the caregiver's memories was not the lack of presents; it was the lack of presence. Her dad was often, neglectfully, under the influence of alcohol while her mom struggled to give her attention.

Material presents cannot replace presence. The best present we can give is presence. I am not against presents; if we can give presents and presence, at the same time on special occasions, then the recipients are blessed. Our parents are mature in their second childhood. Our presence will be the best gift for them, if we have to choose between presents and presence.

11 Gratitude: Great Attitude

If any of us were to stop, rewind our lives and watch things happening to us, we would find many instances where we felt alone and helpless. During some of these times, we thought illogically because we were in such a miserable position.

We are still here today, so obviously we got through the times. How did it happen? There is an unseen power in this world, which helped us. Whether it was another person coming in at the most opportune time, or an idea presenting itself, time and time again, something saved us. Our lives are full of situations where we were pulled out of the darkest places by *something*.

Somehow, we tend to forget these times. We usually just put them aside and get on with our routines. When we do come back to these times, it is usually to complain about them. We need to revisit the memories to consider the unseen force that has saved us so often.

As mentioned earlier in this book, my family and I experienced a near tragic event, which changed my life. On February 16th of 2009, I was shopping for a new car and I soon found the deal of a lifetime.

I quickly agreed to purchase the car and during the weekend, it found its way to me. My friend and I took the Lexus for a drive. We played with the gadgets, agreeing the best feature was the keyless ignition button.

We came home late. The baby was already asleep, and my wife was reading a story to my older son. The day had ended normally.

Tuesday morning began as usual. In recent months, my wife was working with one of my patients two mornings each week. I needed a female therapist for this patient, and my wife was perfect for the job.

My wife had to get going and I was going to spend quality time with my kids until she got back. I would head to the office later that day. I recall making eye contact with my wife, as we laughed about how excited our son was over his bottle. His legs were kicking and his thrill was so evident that it brought smiles to our faces. We said goodbye to one another and then she set off to leave.

My wife shouted to me from the garage. "Manish, the car is not starting!"

"Honey, I am feeding the baby. Did you forget how to use the keyless ignition? I showed you three times." I smiled at our son. Looking at him made me feel more patient.

"I seriously tried everything you told me."

"Just try one more time, dear...."

I heard shouts of frustration as she returned to the garage. She called me again. I rolled my eyes, put the baby down and headed downstairs.

She met me in the kitchen and I walked behind her to the garage. We have 4 steps leading into the garage. I saw her stumble on one of them; I thought she had just missed a step, so I teased her about it. In hindsight, I realize that stumble was the first sign of trouble.

I got into the car and my wife was standing next to me. I began fiddling with the car and repeatedly tried to push the 'engine start' button. Nothing happened. Suddenly, I felt like I was in a movie. My wife, who had just been to the left of me, was not there. My head seemed to turn in slow motion to where she had been standing. I looked down and saw her on the floor. I quickly got out of the car. She was awake and alert, but for some reason, she was not getting off the floor.

"Honey, what happened?"

"I have no idea. I lost my strength."

She tried to get up but could not. It was as if her muscles turned to jelly. I picked her up and helped her back into the house. She did not seem to have energy to make the trip easy.

I wondered what the heck to do next. I had passed my initial reaction to call 911 because she was alert. I figured she was just tired. She had probably skipped breakfast. Could this be why she felt so weak? A million thoughts ran through my mind, I could not organize them all.

I went to get some water. I felt a massive headache coming on. My heart was beating so hard that I could hear it. I was more stressed than I thought. Beginning to panic, I decided to take my wife to the hospital. I told her I was going to call 911. She stopped me.

"You're not calling 911. I'm okay. Look, I am having a normal conversation with you. I am fine."

My son began to cry. I went upstairs to get him, with the glass of water still in my hand. My 4-year-old son came down too. I felt the need to see all of my family at once, together, to ensure their safety. I called AAA next. The dispatcher told me that someone would soon come to start my car.

After that, I called my brother-in-law. He had a medical background and my wife would be comfortable with him. I hoped he would be able to help my wife, and help me stop panicking.

I asked my wife how she was doing. She nodded at me and tried to smile. Not knowing what to do, I checked her blood pressure. She was 98/52, which in general is low, but it was normal for her. I tried to assure myself that she was fine.

I went to the kitchen for something to do to help the situation. I wondered about my headache and heart palpitations. Next, I heard a huge crash. My wife was lying behind me on the tile floor, barely moving.

"Honey, how did this happen?"

"I tried to come to the kitchen on my own but I could not hold myself up."

Panic reached new heights. I picked her off the floor and I took the little one upstairs. Just then, I heard the doorbell; it was a man from AAA. I was relieved to see him.

I tried to ignore my headache, as he tried to jump-start the car. He had a hard time getting it started. I sat in my car with closed doors as my headache worsened. I felt more palpitations. The AAA guy brought in a huge industrial-size battery because he could not start the car with a regular one. He mentioned he had never had to use a battery of this size for any car.

Our chat made for a great distraction from my headache. I told him about my wife passing out this morning and I was feeling ill. He wished me luck, but looked concerned.

Finally the car started and we noticed there was only a quarter tank of gas. I told him this was odd since I had just filled the tank. Panic followed.

"If the car was left on all night, this could all be a result of carbon monoxide poisoning."

"Carbon monoxide poisoning?"

He replied, "Yes. I am sure it is. You should call 911 immediately."

Carbon monoxide is a silent killer. People die sleeping. People that do not die can remain brain-dead or handicapped. I pieced together the reality of what he had said. I thought of my wife fainting, my splitting headache, and my children.

"Oh my God!"

I did what I should have done earlier; call 911. The fire department, police and ambulances arrived. Using specialized detectors and monitors, they entered my home. The machines revealed high carbon monoxide levels. We evacuated the house immediately.

Thank God I was not alone. My brother-in-law was already taking care of the kids, and soon three of my neighbors, all nurses, came as well. My neighbor Jose had just come home from his night shift. He quickly offered to take my kids and brother-in-law to his house.

The paramedics checked my wife, as she lay on the driveway. I refused to be admitted to the hospital. Instead, I got into the ambulance with my wife. While inside, I had no idea what to do to help my wife, but the paramedics looked at me with so much hope and kindness that I felt better. I tried to remember that God helps us at all times that we need help. He is always with us.

One of the paramedics put an oxygen mask over my mouth. I looked out of the window and thought of the times that I had sent patients away in ambulances. I closed my eyes for a moment and tried to think, but all I could do was feel. I could feel the sirens in my body. I felt them racing through my brain. I could feel panic.

Friends, family and neighbors met us at the hospital. My wife was admitted, but the doctors soon decided that she needed to be shifted to another facility, which was better equipped to handle her case because of her high carbon monoxide level. The doctors needed a hyperbaric chamber to continue treatment.

The doctors recommended that I also be admitted because of my severe headache and palpitations. I was on a bed during the initial admission process. I asked them if they would keep my wife and me in the same room. I was more worried about my wife, at that moment, and I could not think of myself. They were not sure if we could room together, so I got up from the bed and rushed to my wife's side. I wanted to be with her.

The doctors tried, a second time, to admit me, especially since I was very emotional. They put me on the same bed, again, to initiate treatment. I thought about my kids and their safety. I knew they were safe with my brother-in-law, but at this point, he called. Before I could update him on what was going on, he dropped a huge bomb.

"We're still with the kids, but the four-year old started vomiting. We're going to bring him into the hospital."

I could not speak, with no idea how to react. I wanted to fall to the ground. It was the worst news I could hear. The doctors were still trying to admit me, but I refused even more with the added news of my kid's situation. My love and affection for my family was so strong, that I could not part with them, even to help myself. Most parents would do the same thing when we need them. They would sacrifice their own safety to find safety for us.

I told my brother-in-law to bring my kids to the next hospital where doctors were sending us. I was still in the lobby of the first hospital when doctors told me that my kids would have to be taken to a children's hospital since this was a critical situation. This was so shocking that I could not imagine being separated from my kids as my wife and I were put in hyperbaric chambers.

After our first round of treatment, we asked to be taken to our kids. We were treated as a special case, and transported to them. It had been ten hours since we saw them, but it felt like ten years has passed us by.

Seeing my son with a mask over his head was too much for me to bear. As I watched them strap him down and prepare for treatment, I tried to grasp what was happening. Through the chaos, I sought and found strength and comfort from my family and friends. Many had left work the moment they heard the news of our challenges. Though my parents were in India, they made it a point to make sure I knew I was not alone.

The waiting rooms filled with friends and family, all sharing positive thoughts, love and prayers. Not only were they all there for me physically, they were also there emotionally. They made it a point to share in my concern. Despite the anxious looks on their faces, they all kept positive attitudes, and I found my strength in them. Looking back, it was a beautiful thing.

I could be upset that my family had to go through this, that we did not hear the car running overnight slowly poisoning us. But I am not upset. With help of family, friends and positive thoughts, I found comfort and peace, knowing God protected us from a near- deadly mistake.

In the end, I walked away feeling gratitude for my family's survival, and the fact that I could celebrate life and love once again. I am truly a changed man from this experience because I see the effects of the invisible power of love and God in my life.

To this day, I cannot fully understand the enormity of what took place on February 16th. We have all had awful things happen to us; we should look at them as positive experiences since we overcame the obstacles. We emerged better and stronger people.

It is not easy, but I always remember to stop, take a deep breath and thank God for everything that He has done for my family and me. I faithfully believe that God saved us for a reason. This incident was the spark to enlighten my spiritual quotient to complete this book.

One day, when I share this incident with my children, they will be able to see the hand of God, and the power of love and friendship that helped us make it through difficult times.

I thank the heroes and angels in my life, which stood by us through difficulty. One day, my sons will be able to thank them. This story will motivate them to be angels and heroes in other people's lives. Without family and friends, I am not sure I would have survived that day when carbon monoxide threatened our lives.

I will share this undying gratitude with my children so they learn that relationships are key to healthy survival. Make gratitude your attitude, if you have not already.

As we know, God is great. He protects us at every turn and moment in our life. We can show our gratitude to God by respecting and loving our parents in their second childhood.

12 Pass Time: Pastime

There is a saying, "some people kill time, some waste time, some use time, but very few invest time." Many seniors are at a loss for what to do with their time, once they retire. But if we understand life well, we realize that even in old age, we have a chance to invest our time in many things. The journey of life continues whether we want it to or not; now is not the time to pass time by feeling sorry for being old.

With much gained experience and wisdom, seniors have an enormous amount to contribute to humanity. They can spend more time with family, cultivating culture into their lives. They may share with family, giving them love, affection and care. They have more time to dedicate to guarantee a healthy, strong bridge between the generations.

If we look to tradition, people have, in all cultures, referred to elders as the ones who are senior to everyone else in terms of experience, understanding, knowledge, and the ability to pass those things on with love. Seniors are in a position to share qualities, not just worldly things such as bank balances, property, and assets. They often have a lot of emotional and intellectual familiarity in society.

No longer seen as just parents to their children, seniors can offer positive support beyond their immediate circle of friends, family, and loved ones. I am not suggesting that seniors take control of their children's lives and dictate every move that they make. Parents must be careful not to become hurdles in their children's journeys to prosperity. Rather, parents should offer understanding and insight, when needed, full of empathy, and working to maintain a strong bond to their children. Parents should see no less than greatness in children, because every person on this planet is divine. The way we behave with people will be the way they respond to us.

Instead of passing time feeling bad about aging, accept old age as pastime. A pastime is defined as an activity that is pursued during spare time. It is the time when we can follow through on all those things we put off for later. It's a time where idleness will not creep into life in any way, shape, or form.

Parents spend so much time and energy on family that it can be difficult to find time for friends, interests, and self. Senior time is when parents no longer nurture children. It is a great time to give back to society. Whether it is giving to a church, temple or social community, we can meet with people and work on ways to improve humankind. We all know people who have great potential. We can tap into each other's potential to make the world a better place in which to live.

Old age should not come with the "I cannot" defense. There are endless ways to remain sharp and insightful. Take this as an opportunity to stop expecting the worst and start seeing the best in all individuals and instances. Try to see what we have rather than what we have not. Your children are the first part of your contributing legacy to the world. Be a part of their lives in a positive way.

13 $SQ=IQ+EQ$

SECOND CHILDHOOD | 122 | Manish Patel

I realized from personal experience that IQ (intelligent quotient) is not the only important life quotient. I feel SQ (spiritual) and EQ (emotional) are just as important as IQ because they help us to find intimacy with God and our loved ones.

Why do people listen to Joel Osteen, Joyce Meyer and other popular spiritual leaders, and feel connected to them? It is because the speakers have high SQ and EQ levels that promote intimate relationships with large groups of people. Love, acceptance, and optimism shine through these speakers and people feel that positive energy that comes from their goodwill to humanity.

This same love, acceptance and optimism shone through my friend, Shreeraj and my patient, Marie. I imagined the concepts greatly benefiting aging parents. Both, Shreeraj and Marie, had high EQ and SQ, which helped them love everyone around them. In their remaining days, when they became dependent, they kept their same beautiful smiles and accepted their dependencies, as would a little child. Aging parents might need to accept their dependency in the same way.

Nothing positive comes from abandoning your parents, if they live to an elderly age and require help with everyday life. Negative deeds produce negative results. Anger, fear, insecurities, and other destructive emotions fasten negativity to us, while causing metaphorical deaths in our lives.

Of course there will be trying times, as it's not always easy to think positive thoughts. So, it's important to find ways to bring positive energy into our lives. Regular streams of positive action feed healthy minds, bodies, and spirits. By controlling our emotions, how we react to life, we reach a higher EQ level.

Concern for humanity is a wonderful way to cycle positive energy. If you want love in your life, practice love for someone else and it will come back to you. If you make another person smile, even just a little, it can do wonders for your mood on a bad day. That is how love, acceptance and optimism work. What you give will find its' way back to you.

It can be fulfilling to provide another person with something. Chasing material brings nothing worthwhile at the end of our lives. If health fails, all the nice things in the world will not save us. In the end, I'd rather have loved ones surrounding me. If you want love in your life, build relationships. Love can heal us. We can turn a bad day into a good one, save a life, and make someone's day. By acting on that love in an emotionally logic manner, we reach a higher SQ level.

There are times when we feel we cannot catch a break. We do not know where to turn for strength or positive people, places, and things. Many people turn to self-help books for inspiration.

Some people read to clear the mind, and settle worries. They tend to find something in books that brings peace to them. As much as I would like this book to be something beautiful that people will want to turn to, I would primarily like this book to bring questions to mind. I want people to think about the concepts of family, angels, heroes, and second childhood as well as the love that Shreeraj showed to all. I want people to find determination through intellectual conviction to stay on quest to become better people.

The concepts of parenting and family hold much weight and value; I am surprised so many people have forgotten this. Great eastern thinker, Shri Pandurang Shastri Athavale said something that struck a chord with me, during one of his lectures, "Let us ensure that while becoming first class doctors, lawyers, professionals we do not become third class family members."

Reevaluate the Qs. Strengthen EQ, IQ and SQ. What we leave behind is more than a square, engraved plaque on a plot of dirt. It is something that finds its' way into the lives of everyone around us, something that has its own energy and life. It is our human spirit.

14 Friend In Deed: Friend Indeed

In this book's inspiration, I talked about my best friend Shreeraj. I will never forget him. The loss of a best friend is always traumatic and it can be difficult to bounce back from such loss.

That first day I was in Mangalore, I recall walking behind Shreeraj to his room, on my way to become his newest roommate. Mangalore was a large and busy city, and I was terrified. Shreeraj calmed me as he carried my two heavy bags into our room.

When he shook my hand, I felt like I was meeting an old friend, and I realized this was a man older than his years. He was someone who I could look to for the rest of the time that I would know him. Soon, I realized that he had the same vision as me: to live for a higher purpose. He hoped to change the world for better. It was through his example and friendship that I learned this is possible.

While writing Second Childhood, I thought about the good times with Shreeraj. I wished I could sit down to share this project, and also share how grateful I am to have met him. I wish I could repay him for all that he has done for me.

I have lived on 2 continents and I have met hundreds of people in my travels. But, never have I met anyone as selfless and kind as Shreeraj.

Shreeraj was gifted at Anatomy. His father was an Anatomy Professor at a top medical school in India. Shreeraj inherited his father's learning gift; he was the top student in our class.

One day, our Anatomy teacher posed quite a complex question. Usually, Shreeraj answered the questions that stumped the rest of us. We all turned to him for the answer, but he was also stumped. Instead of learning the concept from books, like the rest of us, Shreeraj decided to make a 600-mile trip to learn from his father. He considered his father the perfect teacher.

The concept did not matter much to the rest of us, so we were satisfied to learn the basics from the book and allow Shreeraj to teach us when he returned to school. He was a perfectionist, a good student, and a better teacher. No matter what the question, Shreeraj always answered it in a way that helped us to forever apply the concept.

Even after Shreeraj's diagnosis, his great attributes radiated out of him. His life was just as enthusiastic, in the end, as it was when I first met him. He continued to work and help others without worry for his welfare. He was able to stay cool and calm, even in worst situations.

It was Shreeraj's personality, which made his eventual passing easier for him and for those around him. It was as if we were leaning on him for comfort even though he was the one dying.

I never saw him miserable or angry when we were younger, or when he was older and ill. I never saw him cry or approach a situation without a cool and balanced head.

He had an amazing relationship with all of those around him, especially his family. He helped his sister get in to the university that we attended. His role was integral in her earning a degree in Fashion Design and Art. He was her emotional and mental support any time she needed it. Now that I look back, I am amazed by the amount of maturity and strength he had to carry so many of us on his shoulders, during his teenage years.

My wife, son and I went to India to visit my family, and also to spend time with Shreeraj after his diagnosis. Shreeraj and I decided to visit our old medical college. My wife and son remained behind with Shreeraj's wife and son.

After the visit to the college, I accompanied Shreeraj to see his Oncologist. While waiting for the doctor, we did not have much to do except people watch. Everyone seemed to be burdened with panic and depression. They seemed aware of their reality as cancer patients. I cannot say that I blamed them for looking scared. If I had cancer, I would feel the same way. When I turned toward Shreeraj, he seemed to be at peace. He was the only person that I knew who could enjoy life in an oncologist's waiting room.

Shreeraj seemed to turn his doctor's mood around. The doctor greeted him like he was his best friend, with open arms and a smile. Shreeraj's effect on people was amazing. If you saw the interaction between them, without hearing the conversation, you would not guess Shreeraj was preparing to undergo chemotherapy. It was as if the two men were about to enjoy a cup of tea.

During Shreeraj's visit, the doctor said he was doing better than anyone had expected. He had barely lost any weight, despite chemotherapy. The forecast had been Shreeraj would survive for a few months after his diagnosis. Several months passed, and Shreeraj remained with us.

Fear and doubt were not part of Shreeraj's personality. I think his positive life view kept him alive and healthy during the five years that he survived with cancer. Shreeraj saw cancer as a blessing. He said it was his time to enjoy life to the fullest. He wanted to speak to as many friends as possible. He wanted to meet as many new people as possible. He wanted to get in the world and continue living as if nothing was wrong.

I could see Shreeraj accepting his second childhood with grace and optimism, when he became dependent, despite the fact that he was only 34 years old. He is a prime example that accepting the reality of a situation does not have to be a bad thing. He embraced it and was able to work with it to ensure nothing went wrong. Things always improved for those around him, no matter how little the change. It is this unconditional love and selfless intentions that improve the world.

Shreeraj not only survived after his terminal diagnosis; he thrived. He did this using a positive outlook and sheer mental strength. Shreeraj had become the embodiment of human love. It was part of his spirit, and because of this, he was able to face cancer head-on. This improved his well-being, and the well being of those around him.

I often wondered about the magic Shreeraj had inside of him. What was it that made him so special? How could he be so positive, mature and influential as he battled such a deadly sickness?

Shreeraj fought negative situations by using positive thoughts to overcome them. We all know that negative thoughts are harmful and disruptive. As a result, we should not let them enter our minds. Do your best to follow Shreeraj's example and keep joy in your life so that negativity cannot enter, no matter what the circumstance.

Every year, I deal with hundreds of patients. The majority of those who suffer from cancer, or deadly disease, show signs of fear and insecurity. However, Shreeraj lived a mentally and spiritually outstanding life, despite being diagnosed with an incurable illness. If he could give people love and support, despite everything he was going through, why can we not do the same for people? Our efforts *can* improve people's standards of life.

Shreeraj taught me that the world could be a better place if we love each other selflessly. He proved this by being a friend to everyone with whom he came into contact. He passed no judgment; he was, indeed, a friend in deed.

Shreeraj was like a child, in positive ways. Children do not hold grudges. They forgive and love us despite our shortcomings. It's time that we learn to be this way as adults. By letting go of the small, futile things, life will become exponentially enjoyable. By reflecting on his life, we see that we have an important part to play in this world. We could put a smile on someone's face, or become such a positive influence to inspire someone to write a book!

There are times when we have not spoken properly to our family and loved ones. Perhaps we have not been there for them as much as we should have been, or could have been. Whatever feelings we have bottled up inside, these are the times to begin letting them out. We must take advantage of this life. Start doing the things that we can, while we still have a chance.

For giving love, do not worry about what we receive in return. Sooner or later, the blessings that accompany any good deed will turn up in life.

Blessings slowly add up, day by day, and gradually improve our little corner of the universe. Good deeds improve our thoughts and demeanor, which in turn improve the thoughts and demeanor of those around us. We soon find positive energy and light pervading all things. Our quality of life and mind seem to effortlessly improve.

It is these blessings that pave the way to bring more beautiful things into our lives and the lives of those around us. This place of God and love is the ideal setting for us to begin our journey into our second parenthood and second childhood.

Shreeraj set this example for all of us: he found time to love someone else, and we should do the same. Love all those around you, especially your parents, while you still have the chance.

Before and after cancer diagnosis, Shreeraj helped many cancer patients. It broke my heart to think of him laying in the same ICU where he had treated patients in his role as a cardio pulmonary physical therapist.

I could not be with him during his last days, but his family told me that he tried to communicate using sign language, when he was no longer able to speak. Shreeraj developed septicemia, which led to multiple-organ failure. He had multiple tubes passing through his mouth, preventing speech. In spite of this, he managed to communicate with his wife, parents, and 7-year old son.

One day, he pointed his finger at the letters, ICU, telling his family that he saw God. Shreeraj used the intensive care unit acronym to reveal its deeper meaning - I see you, and I see God in you, too. My friend, Shreeraj, you do not know what you have given to me. I promise to keep you alive, forever in our hearts. You will always be missed.

15 It Is Not The End. It Is The Beginning.

Often, we sleep after reading a book, but I want this book to be a wake-up alarm. We may have tried to snooze relationships many times, but the only way we can turn this alarm off is by taking a step to improve relationships with loved ones. As I worked on this project, I saw a positive difference in my attitude to my parents, spouse, and kids.

I am confident that my readers can enjoy their life at any age. Second Childhood would never be complete if I had not received special blessings from God. Some of those blessings came in the form of "priceless hugs" like the one I received at Bishop Park of Detroit, Michigan.

After losing Shreeraj, when I thought of this book, it did not seem possible to accomplish this task with my busy schedule as a therapist. But when I mentioned these thoughts to my patients, they encouraged me to write this book; and they provided moral support for me to complete it.

In one of my more recent radio interviews, the host shared a powerful story, which I would like to share with you. The radio host had a friend, who was living with his wife, mother, and young child. The child was close to his grandma, but the friend's wife did not like the mother-in-law in the house. His wife wanted to put grandma in a home.

When the couple discussed nursing home options, the grandson opposed. But the decision was already made, and one day they dropped grandma off to a nursing home, against the tears of little grandson and grandma.

Driving home, the child started drawing a map. The mother asked what he was doing. Her son told her that he was drawing a map to make sure that he could remember the nursing home location to bring his mom and dad when they got old. This is a great example of how our children model our behavior.

We need to pause in life and re-evaluate our portfolio. We make financial investments by expecting 6 to 8 % return, but when we invest in relationships, there is a chance for infinite growth. Once you understand and appreciate the concept of second childhood, I want you to explain it to your parents and loved ones. Let them know dependency is not a curse, it is blessing because some people do not live up to a dependent age. Prepare to be a better parent to your parents. Teach your children to love and care for elders.

If you can make one person feel love, then you can make the whole world feel it. If you have not spoken to your parents for a long time, then please call them or walk into their home and heart to show your gratitude toward them. After you read Second Childhood, should you like to share your experience with me, visit thesecondchildhood.com and send me a note.

About Manish Patel

I consider myself to be an eternal student, as I love dialogue. I love listening to, and sharing with, patients (most are seniors), family, friends, and the people I have been fortunate enough to build relationships with in life. I do not think I have fully become the person I want to be, but I am on my way. My effort is genuine.

SECOND CHILDHOOD | 144 | Manish Patel

When the idea of writing Second Childhood clicked in my mind's mirror, I was totally occupied by universal source. At the time, my life's events were happening like chapters in a book. I received wisdom to correlate the incidences with words that flowed from the super conscious to my conscious mind. My pen and recorder kept running as God used my hand and voice as instruments to create Second Childhood.

Along this journey I learned great things. I have grown as a son, husband and a father to my children.

It was not possible for me to meet each of you to discuss this beautiful concept of second childhood, so I decided to talk to you through this book. Take this concept to your loved ones, and tell them that dependency is not a curse.

God wants us to be children again. There is no shame when children take help from someone. Tell them to embrace dependency with grace and enjoy it. And, make sure you are the best parent for your parents.

God Bless You.
Manish Patel

TheSecondChildhood.com

Made in the USA
Charleston, SC
28 November 2011